MACK® BUSES 1900 THROUGH 1960

PHOTO ARCHIVE

Edited with introduction by
Harvey Eckart

Iconografix
Photo Archive Series

Iconografix
PO Box 446
Hudson, Wisconsin 54016 USA

Iconografix books are offered at a discount when sold in quantity for promotional use. Businesses or organizations seeking details should write to the Marketing Department, Iconografix, at the above address.

Library of Congress Card Number: 99-76049

ISBN 1-58388-020-8

00 01 02 03 04 05 06 5 4 3 2 1

Printed in the United States of America

Cover and book design by Shawn Glidden

Copy Editing by Dylan Frautschi

COVER PHOTO: This C49 model bus was typical of the more than 7,000 C model transit buses built after World War II. Citizens Rapid Transit of Hampton, VA received forty-five C47 and C49 buses between 1948 and 1960.

Iconografix Inc. exists to preserve history through the publication of notable photographic archives and the list of titles under the Iconografix imprint is constantly growing. Transportation enthusiasts should be on the Iconografix mailing list and are invited to write and ask for a catalog, free of charge.

Authors and editors in the field of transportation history are invited to contact the Editorial Department at Iconografix, Inc., PO Box 446, Hudson, WI 54016. We require a minimum of 120 photographs per subject. We prefer subjects narrow in focus, e.g., a specific model, railroad, or racing venue. Photographs must be of high quality, suited to large format reproduction.

PREFACE

The histories of machines and mechanical gadgets are contained in the books, journals, correspondence, and personal papers stored in libraries and archives throughout the world. Written in tens of languages, covering thousands of subjects, the stories are recorded in millions of words.

Words are powerful. Yet, the impact of a single image, a photograph or an illustration, often relates more than dozens of pages of text. Fortunately, many of the libraries and archives that house the words also preserve the images.

In the *Photo Archive Series*, Iconografix reproduces photographs and illustrations selected from public and private collections. The images are chosen to tell a story—to capture the character of their subject. Reproduced as found, they are accompanied by the captions made available by the archive.

The Iconografix *Photo Archive Series* is dedicated to young and old alike, the enthusiast, the collector and anyone who, like us, is fascinated by "things" mechanical.

ACKNOWLEDGMENTS

The photographs appearing in this book were made available by the Mack Trucks Historical Museum, and the private collection of the editor.

BIBLIOGRAPHY

Montville, John B., MACK, Aztec Corporation, Tucson, Arizona 1979

MOTOR COACH AGE Mar-Apr Issue 1974

Plachno, Larry, MODERN INTERCITY COACHES, Transportation Trails, Polo, IL. 1997

Mack Allentown, PA, plant 5C was the site of Mack bus production from the late 1920s until the end of Mack transit bus production in 1960. The plant was a beehive of bus building activity at the time of this shot; August, 1947.

INTRODUCTION

Although Mack Trucks Inc. is today known primarily for their medium and heavy-duty truck models, such was not always the case. Throughout their 100-year history of vehicle design and manufacture, a diverse array of products were featured. Rail cars and locomotives were built during the 1920s and 1930s, and truck trailers were made during the 1930s and 1940s. Off-highway mining and construction trucks were marketed as a separate and distinct product line until 1978. Mack custom-built fire apparatus was manufactured until 1990.

Mack is today the oldest surviving U.S. truck builder, but ironically, as frequently stated in Mack advertising literature: "The first Mack was a bus and the first bus was a Mack." In 1900 Isaac Harris had a conversation with Gus Mack regarding the use of motor vehicles in sightseeing service in New York City's Prospect Park. Mack agreed to build a motor bus for Harris, who agreed to purchase it after a satisfactory trial period. Although the exact delivery date is unknown, the first prototype Mack bus was first operated successfully early in the 20th century and sold to Harris. Additional orders for similar units quickly followed, and the first advertisement for a Mack bus appeared in 1903.

Like fire apparatus, bus production played a prominent role in Mack's development, particularly in the 1920s and 1930s. Mack built buses from 1900 to 1960, and during that period produced over 21,000 units, and over 24,000 if school bus chassis and export chassis models are included. These figures are believed to be higher than any other American manufacturer except General Motors, who, in a strange twist of fate, also voluntarily exited the bus manufacturing business; in 1986.

Mack bus production began in Brooklyn, NY. A move to Allentown, PA, in 1905 became the site of both truck and bus production. The trade name "Manhattan" was used for the designs of various buses and the earliest heavy-duty trucks. In the 1920s bus and truck chassis became distinct from each other. In 1943 bus production halted as the U.S. Navy requisitioned the Allentown bus plant for Vultee Aircraft to produce torpedo bombers. Following V-E Day,

Allentown was once again the site of bus production, resuming operations in 1945, and continuing until the final production ended in early 1960. Sidney, OH, was the site for the production of 26 intercity buses in 1958. Mack bought the C. D. Beck Co., Sidney, OH, plant in 1956 in anticipation of a large order for Greyhound, which did not materialize. The production of the newly introduced C model fire apparatus at the Sidney, OH, plant was very successful, and production of this series was moved back to PA after the Sidney plant was closed in late 1958.

During the bus production years, Mack built transit types primarily, with both Mack and vendor supplied bodies. Mack intercity coaches were marketed in three distinct time periods. The AL bus chassis, introduced in 1926, was specifically designed for high speed, intercity service. The first intercity era ended in the late 1930s. In 1958 Mack re-entered the intercity market with a model 97D, which was built in Sidney, OH, and sold a modest 26 units. In 1985 Mack attempted to market a Renault-built intercity coach, the FR-1, which met with such limited success that in 1988, Mack again disbanded its bus operations and repurchased the few FR-1s that were sold.

Mack's transit type bus production can be viewed in several distinct segments: the initial conventional, front motor types built until 1937; transit type, front motor units built from 1931 to 1938; rear motor types built from 1934 to 1943; and the post W.W. II rear motor types built from 1945 to 1960.

The photos that follow are shown mostly in chronological order and include at least one photo of the many different models produced. Noteworthy developments and engineering advances are noted.

Unlike highway trucks and fire apparatus, buses were normally run until their useful life was complete and then scrapped. Relatively few buses have been restored or preserved, which is why I believe this photographic, historical presentation of Mack buses fulfills a long felt need.

The Original Mack Touring Coach, Circa 1900.

"AMERICA'S FIRST BUS·BUILT 1900"

This Mack advertising brochure shot is somewhat misleading as it is not the original Mack bus, but a later one of similar design, which is presently displayed at the Mack Trucks Historical Museum in Allentown, PA. The original Mack bus was built in Brooklyn, NY, and is said to have operated for 17 years for over one million miles in the NYC area. It was powered by a 4-cylinder motor with a top speed of 20 miles per hour. It had a 3-speed transmission, with chain drive and rode on 36-inch wooden artillery type wheels. Mack's reputation for durability and versatility was firmly established by these pioneering vehicles.

This is an ADS-1 bus, first displayed at the American Transit Association convention in St. Louis in 1956. It was Mack's last new transit bus design and was referred to as a "dream bus" or "bus of tomorrow." It never entered production status and the lone Alex de Sakhnoffsky styled prototype was eventually sold to and operated by Schenectady Street Railway in NY. It was later destroyed in a garage fire.

Prior to the introduction of the AB models, over 150 early sightseeing buses were built in both Brooklyn, NY, and Allentown, PA. Few photos of these early buses are available, and this undated photo is very similar, but not identical to the unit on page 8. The passengers appear to be in relatively good spirits.

Although the quality of this undated photo is poor, it does show an early bus with doors, but still lacks windows.

A-1123

AB model buses were produced from the early 1920s to 1934 and were the best selling single models made, with over 3,800 delivered. This 1921 bus was the first "shock insulated" bus built in Allentown, and is referred to as a "hi type." Springs, radiator, and steering gears mounted in rubber bushings comprised the "shock insulated" nomenclature, and this was regarded as a major advancement.

This 1922 city type AB had hard rubber tires and a composite body. A 56 hp 4-cylinder motor provided the motive power.

This 1923 AB is listed as the first "low bus." This new drop frame construction allowed lowering the floor of the bus several inches and accounted for a new surge of business for the Mack AB chassis. Compare the lower body height of this unit to the unit on page 13.

This 1924 AB parlor coach carries the characteristic spelling of "Mack" and the company logo on the sides, as well as the words "performance counts" on the radiator, which was a famous Mack slogan for many years. The rugged fenders, drum headlights, and front shock absorbers are prominent. The customer for this unit was Jefferson Highway Transportation, Minneapolis, MN.

This streamlined 1924 AB parlor car has a Lang body. Lang was a prominent body builder at the time.

Details of the low slung AB bus chassis are shown in this 1924 photo.

This is an AB gas electric chassis, one of 91 built between 1925 and 1930. The Mack motor drove a GE generator, which powered a GE traction motor. The standard AB dual reduction rear axle was used.

18

The AB was available with both Mack-built bodies or those of outside suppliers, such as this 1926 all aluminum body by American Body Co., complete with rooftop storage area. A good number of C style cabs for use on AB and AC trucks are stored in the background.

This fleet shot in 1927 shows 5 ABs with locally built bodies, in the service of Wellington Corp. Tramways in Wellington, New Zealand.

These Mack-built bodies are awaiting transfer to the final assembly line where they will be mated to Mack chassis. Prior to the production of steel bodies in 1932, earlier units were of composite construction.

L.351.
4|6|27.

This 1927 AB parlor coach for Knickerbocker Sightseeing Co., of NYC, is particularly ornate. Whitewall tires and substantial chrome rear bumper are noteworthy.

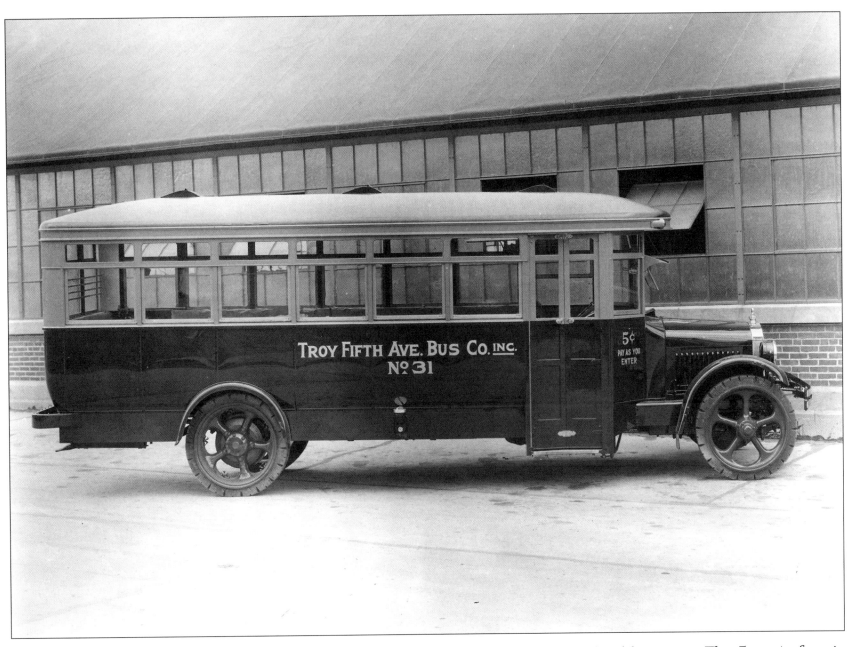

This 1928 AB city bus is one of the last equipped with the bone jarring solid rubber tires. The 5 cents fare is prominently displayed.

This 1928 AB city bus is equipped with a Bender body. This was before the days of rear-view mirrors, turn signals, or clearance lights.

The spartan driver's position in an AB city bus is shown, along with the seat tilted to reveal the tool box complement. The price of a 231 1/4-inch wheelbase AB chassis on Jan. 1, 1930 was $4,750 list, with a Mack body ranging from $3,450 to $3,750 list.

MACK
3½ TON AC CHASSIS. 40 PASS. BUS
#???

The AB was Mack's light and medium duty line and the mighty AC model was the heavy-duty truck model. The AC truck chassis was used for some bus offerings and could well be labeled a classic case of "overkill." This is a 40 passenger bus on a very early 5 1/2-ton AC chassis.

The snub-nosed AC earned Mack the moniker "bulldog" during WWI. AC chassis were produced from 1916 through 1938. The combination of solid tires and brick streets must have produced a hard ride for this 1919 AC enclosed bus.

These three white AC open sightseeing buses appear to be in the service of the same Knickerbocker Co. as the AB shown on page 22. The photo is undated, but the NY license plates bear the year 1920.

MACK AC tractor and trailer which carries 100 people, used by the
Texas Oil Company for transporting their employees.

Tractor-trailer buses are rare but not unheard of. Info on this photo states this AC tractor is pulling a trailer
built by Texas Wagon Works to haul 100 employees of the Texas Oil Co. A real "people mover."

This has to be the most "interesting" photo in this volume. This is a 1924 AP model, experimental 6-cylinder bus chassis, which became known as '"The Mack Great Coach" after being fitted with a body. At the wheel smoking his pipe is Alfred Fellows Masury, Mack's chief engineer from 1914 until 1933, when his tragic death occurred in the crash of the U.S. airship Akron. Masury was a brilliant engineer whose staff kept Mack at the peak of technical excellence. Could the other individuals shown be part of the "AP committee?"

The demand for larger, more powerful bus chassis resulted in an AL 6-cylinder model introduced in late 1926. Over 575 were produced through 1929, including 87 gas electrics. The setting for this photo is obviously a show, where a Lang body is displayed on an AL chassis with low-mounted headlights.

This white 1932 AL sports disc wheels, mounted spare tire, and rooftop storage rack. The AL became a major player in the intercity coach market and presented a sleek, low hood design.

Powering the AL was a 425 cubic-inch 6-cylinder motor with a 4 1/4 by 5-inch bore and stroke. Clearly shown are the multiple heads, updraft carburetor, and firing order stamped on the water distribution jacket.

33

MACK MODEL BC
A COMPACT 90 H.P. BUS THAT PROVI-
DES ECONOMICAL PERFORMANCE BETWEEN
THAT OF THE 4-CYLINDER BUS AND BIG SIX.
AN IDEAL BUS FOR THOSE ROUTES
WHERE TOPOGRAPHICAL CONDITIONS OR
SCHEDULES REQUIRE JUST SOMEWHAT
MORE THAN THE PERFORMANCE ABILITY
OF 4-CYLINDER BUSES.

PHOTO NO.
A-3347

MACK MODEL BC 6-CYLINDER CHASSIS OF 90 H. P. WITH CITY TYPE
BODY. CAPACITY 25 OR 29 PASSENGERS.

ALBUM PAGE
NO. M-1

411 BC 6-cylinder bus models were made between 1929 and 1937, and were promoted to operators that needed more performance than the 4-cylinder models would provide. The BC used a 6-cylinder 404 cubic-inch motor of 90 hp, and a 4-speed transmission.

This 1930 BC city type bus was in the service of The Mastco Co. of Hartford, CT. The list price on Jan. 1, 1930 for a 231 1/4-inch wheelbase BC chassis was $5,550. Capacities ranged from 25 to 33 passengers.

The big 6-cylinder BK bus model was produced from 1929 through 1934 and was the "top dog" of its era. The 1931 bus in this photo is widely known after being restored to original condition by Greyhound in 1972. It is an interstate type with serial number 6BK3S1134, and was originally delivered to Lebanon AutoBus Co. on Sept. 24, 1931. It was considered one of the finest coaches of its day and carried a price tag of approximately $15,250. Called "the galloping ghost," the old 1931 bus now shares the spotlight with several other restored Greyhound antiques.

This 1931 shot poses eight BKs for use by Pickwick Greyhound Lines, who bought 26 Mack interstate buses in 1930 and 1931.

Photographed at a bus show in 1929, this BK chassis was elaborately displayed, including the suspended motor components. The first versions of the BK chassis included a 525 cubic-inch 6-cylinder motor of 122 hp and 346 foot-pounds of torque. An AL 4-speed transmission was used with a rear axle ratio of 4.90.

The BK was primarily an intercity coach, but some of the 544 units built were of the city type coach such as this one with front and rear entrance doors. The photographer, in this case, took great care to pose the unit in front of an elegant house. The Jan. 1, 1930 list price of a BK chassis was $6,600, with air brakes $300 extra, and bodies ranging from $3,950 to $5,500.

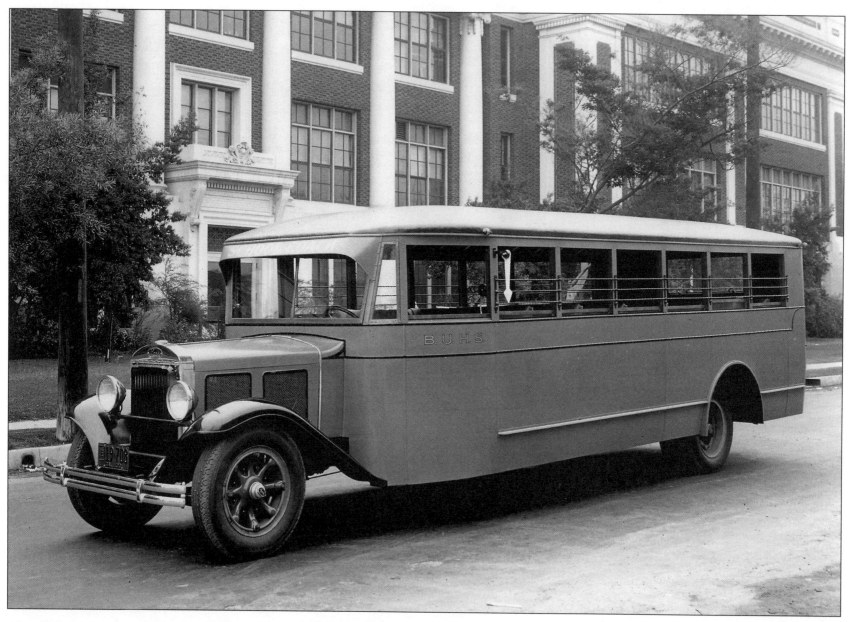

The BG bus was the last of the conventional style buses, introduced in 1931 with 183 produced through 1937. A 309 cubic-inch 6-cylinder motor was used with a 4-speed transmission. This unit was delivered to Brawley Union High School with a 50 passenger Egge school bus body. It had a 231-inch wheelbase and rode on 7:50 by 20 tires.

These two BGs were delivered to Oceanside-Carlsbad Union High School and had similar specs to those on the preceding page, except the body was built by Crown, a Los Angeles, CA, area bus builder.

131-L-5224

The BT, produced from 1931 through 1934 was still front motor driven, but the design was now of the so-called "transit type" rather than the conventional type with a hood out front. This was also the last model with composite body construction, as used on some units. This unit has doors both at the front and extreme rear.

732-L6056

This action shot of a BT with all steel body shows the windshield visor, large non-sealed beam headlights, and prominent radiator grille. Ugly may be too harsh a word, but its boxy styling was definitely not a styling winner. The passengers are decked out in straw hats and bonnets.

One of 87 BTs built is shown under construction. Dual fans cool the 525 cubic-inch 6-cylinder motor. I'm not sure if the worker shown behind the front wheel is hard at work or taking a nap.

932 A5232 A

441 CLs were built between 1932 and 1937. Similar to the BT in appearance, they were smaller, seating 30 instead of 42 or 44, and used a smaller 468 cubic-inch 6-cylinder motor.

734A6010

This two-tone CL utilizes a single front entrance door.

CLs on the production line in the spacious 5C plant in 1933.

932A5240A

Shown on this CL are the driver position, spartan interior, and hood cover removed. A 4-speed transmission and air brakes were supplied.

CG-1234A6199

Only 76 CGs were built from 1933 through 1937. This uniquely positioned 1934 photo shows the undercarriage. Only a 3-speed transmission was used on these smaller units. Power was supplied by a small 310 cubic-inch 6-cylinder BG motor.

CG-934A6087

This CG poses sans its outer skin.

CG-934A6098

The CG was the smallest bus built by Mack. It was under 23 feet in length and had 20 seats.

Trolley buses were built from 1934 through 1943. This 1943 CR is one of 275 made, along with 15 FR models. Portland Traction Co. was Mack's largest trolley coach customer at 141 units.

The substantial Westinghouse electrical equipment is neatly placed in the rear compartment of this 1938 CR model delivered to Kansas City Public Service in Kansas City, MO.

CR-1234A6194

This 1934 photo of a CR chassis shows the maze of electrical components, and their accompanying electrical conduits.

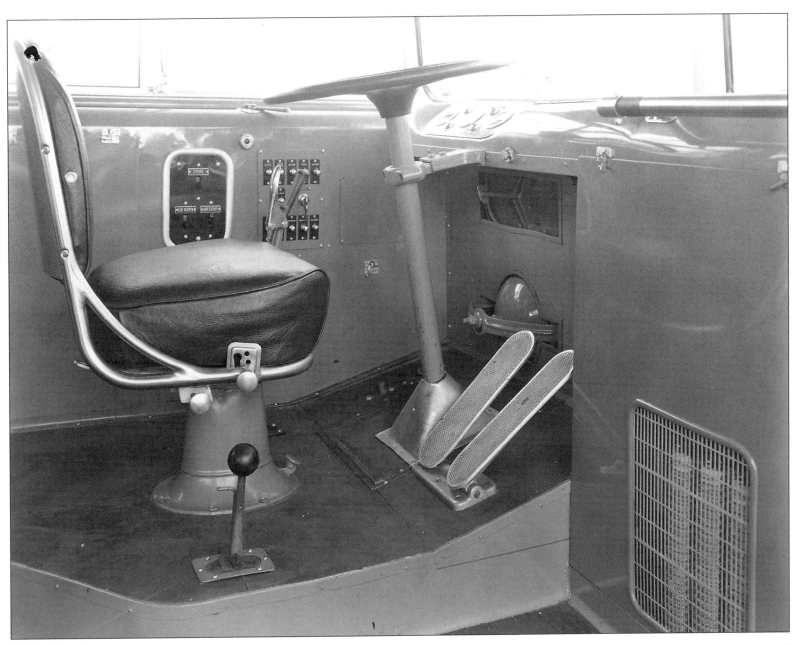

The operator's area is quite neat and simple. Of course, no clutch pedal is needed. The first CR was delivered to Dorr Street line, Toledo, OH, in early 1935.

The first transit bus with a rear motor was the CQ model, introduced in 1934. 886 were built through 1941. This 1938 unit with front and center doors was delivered to Montgomery Bus Corp., Jersey City, NJ.

The 8th Street bridge in Allentown was a frequent background for photos. Shown is a fleet of four CQ, 30 passenger transit type buses delivered to Long Beach Bus Co. Inc., Long Beach, NY.

A 1937 CQ before application of exterior "skin."

Details of the placement of the motor, radiator, and right angle drive transmission in a CQ chassis are shown, along with a shot of the dash and operating controls. CQs used a 468 or 525 cubic-inch, 6-cylinder L-head motor and a 3-speed transmission.

More modern styling is evident in this 1936 CQ model delivery to Pittsburgh Motor Coach Co., in PA, although the contribution of the rear wheel skirts is questionable. The park background is a nice touch.

CT-635A6490

The larger 35 to 39 passenger CT was built from 1935 through 1942 with 574 made. This 1935 unit was delivered to Boston Elevated Railway. The 535 cubic-inch gasoline motor was standard, but in 1938 the Mack Hercules powered diesel bus was introduced, with the first two CT-4D diesel electric models also going to Boston.

This 1937 CT was one of ten delivered to Motor Transit Co., Los Angeles, CA. The compartments and fancy paint job are unusual. Mack supplied the shell and frame only, and Crown Motor Carriage Works of Los Angeles, CA, provided the balance of the body and interior hardware. Crown, like Mack, built both buses and fire apparatus, each with a loyal base of customers, but Crown closed its doors in 1991.

The CW, 20 to 25 passenger bus was built from 1935 through 1941 and was a popular model with 1,310 made. This 1936 unit was delivered to Boro Buses Corp. in Red Bank, NJ.

This 1935 CW is obviously undergoing a test for water leaks outside the plant. This 20 passenger model was delivered to Utah Light and Traction Co., Salt Lake City, UT.

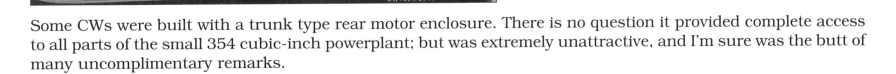

Some CWs were built with a trunk type rear motor enclosure. There is no question it provided complete access to all parts of the small 354 cubic-inch powerplant; but was extremely unattractive, and I'm sure was the butt of many uncomplimentary remarks.

The CY was produced from 1937 through 1941 with 329 built. The 354 cubic-inch 6-cylinder motor and 3-speed transmission were used. This 1938 unit was delivered to East Street Bus Lines Inc., New Britain, CT.

Prominent in this photo of a CY interior are the multiple wipers, long gear-shift lever, period type fare box, and intrusive spare tire and rim.

The E series truck chassis was extensively used for school bus units. This 1939 model 43SB is equipped with a Superior all steel body. Mack built 756 school bus chassis between 1936 and 1942.

The CM model was produced from 1939 through 1942, and was second only to the AB as Mack's most popular pre-WWII bus model with 1,877 built. Shown are exterior and interior views of a highway post office, as used in this era.

An impressive fleet photo of twenty 1941 CMs for Akron Transportation Co., Akron, OH.

Shown are detailed views of the CM motor, drive train, and rear axle.

This 1941 CM was delivered to Mill Valley Transit. Lighting equipment includes non-sealed beam headlights, fog lamps, clearance and marker lights, and a spotlight. Only one tiny rear-view mirror is evident.

This CM shell shows provision for both a front and rear door opening. 40 to 44 passenger capacities were available. This is a unified body structure in which the body framing, of high tensile steel, is interlocked with the chassis to form a single structural unit.

The EP, 611 cubic-inch, overhead valve, gasoline motor is shown with updraft carburetor. The 611 was widely used in CM and CO bus models and type 80 fire apparatus. The CM was also the first Mack bus model to use the Mack ED diesel bus motor of 519 cubic-inch displacement, which developed 131 hp.

Notably absent from this driver area in a CM is a clutch pedal. The CM used a newly introduced air operated automatic clutch, which was activated by moving the gear-shift lever and throttle pedal. A synchromesh transmission was used and this combination proved to be both sturdy and reliable in use.

This handsome 1939 CM suburban type bus was delivered to Trenton and Lambertville Bus Lines Inc. in Trenton, NJ.

The CO model was a slightly smaller version of the CM and 165 were produced between 1939 and 1942. This 1939 CO was an Atlantic General Division demonstrator.

The rear shot of this 1939 CO demonstrator shows the extensive rear cooling louvers.

350 L25s were built between 1939 and 1941. This was a light-duty bus of 23 to 25 passenger capacity with a tiny 290 cubic-inch Continental 6-cylinder motor, and 3-speed transmission. This 1939 single door L25 was one of many sold locally to the Lehigh Valley Transportation Co. Both Boyertown and Bender supplied some L25 bodies.

The neat interior of an L25 is shown. The dash speedometer is the same as used in the E series trucks of the same era. The L25 used vacuum over hydraulic brakes rather than air, as used on the heavier models.

503 LCs were built from 1940 through 1943 and were of medium-duty with 31 passenger capacity. This 1940 LC with period type turn signals and reflectors was delivered to Albany Transit Co., Albany, NY.

This 1940 LC is outfitted with rear wheel skirts and large cooling cutouts rather than the customary louvers. An EN457 motor was standard with the EN510 as an option.

Only one experimental CD model was built in 1940. This was a big 48 passenger coach with an ED diesel motor and electric drive. It had a 268-inch wheelbase and was offered for sale in 1941 for $12,400.

A second one-of-a-kind CP experimental model was built in 1942. It was a 27 passenger model. A single, truck type rear-view mirror is shown.

371 LDs were built between 1941 and 1943. They were 35 to 39 passenger capacity and used the EN510 motor of 150 hp. This was the first LD built.

172 RBs were built in 1941 and 1942. These medium-duty 27 passenger buses used the smaller EN354 motor of 116 hp. This fog light equipped unit was delivered to Boro Buses Corp. of Red Bank, NJ.

190 RC models were built in 1941 and 1942. These 31 to 35 passenger buses used the EN354 motor. The FOB Allentown, PA, price of an RC in 1941 was $7,100.

Only 14 KB models were built in 1941 and 1942. This was the lightest-duty bus available at the time, and it used a small EN330 motor. This is the first KB built, and it was delivered to the Lovell Bus Lines in MA.

Between 1941 and 1950 Mack built over 1,600 units designated CBA through CBL forward control chassis. The CB stood for "conventional bus." The majority were principally for export to Central America and Europe, with some sold to U.S. customers under school bus bodies. Shown here is a 1949 CBL with both front and rear entrances.

A 1949 CBL chassis is shown. The majority were equipped with gasoline motors, but 326 were equipped with diesel motors between 1947 and 1950.

Post WWII production began in 1945 with the C41, which was built through 1957, and except for the AB, was Mack's best selling bus at 2,357 units. 1,542 were gasoline powered and 815 were diesels. Shown here is a pilot model and the second bus equipped with a torque converter transmission. The motor was an EN672 gasoline unit of 189 hp.

C233

All postwar buses were to be equipped with torque converter drive, but an air operated gear-shift mechanism was used prior to March 1947. Shown here is the Spicer-built torque converter. Reports indicate these were high maintenance items with leaks being a major problem.

This 1950 C41DT (DT for diesel, torque converter) was highly modified for security reasons for the U.S. Immigration and Naturalization Service. Disc wheels were specified.

The postwar C bus series was attractively styled, as is this 1954 C41DT for Ave. B and East Broadway Transit Co. Inc. of NYC. This is part of an order for 10 buses. Sealed beam headlights were now standard. Also shown are arrow type turn signals and the attractive emblem, as used on some postwar buses and C model fire apparatus.

A parking problem is evident as Allentown plant SC is in full swing bus production as shown in this 1946 photo. The plant totaled 11 1/2 acres. Shown is position 59 for check up, final adjustment, and special installations.

The C45 model was produced from 1947 through 1954 with over 1,900 units built. This heavy-duty 45 passenger bus is equipped with a Mack END672 diesel motor of 165 hp. This motor was first offered in larger capacity buses during 1948, and later used in heavy-duty Mack truck models. During the early and mid-fifties, two of Mack's principal competitors, ACF Brill and White, quit building buses. GM remained Mack's most formidable competitor.

C45GT3519-1247C 2113

This single door C45GT is being loaded for rail shipment to the Sinclair Refining Co. of Houston, TX. The EN672 gasoline motor used in this bus had a 25 higher horsepower rating than the END672 diesel.

Allentown plant 5C is shown in this 1947 photo, showing position 61 for check up after road test run. Mack built 2,408 buses in 1947, the highest year ever. Also shown in the aisle are E series truck chassis.

C33GT1026-748C2843

Mack delivered 59 C33 buses between 1948 and 1951. This 33 passenger bus was the smallest post WWII bus offered. The 1948 C33 shown had a short 180-inch wheelbase and was a Southern Division demonstrator.

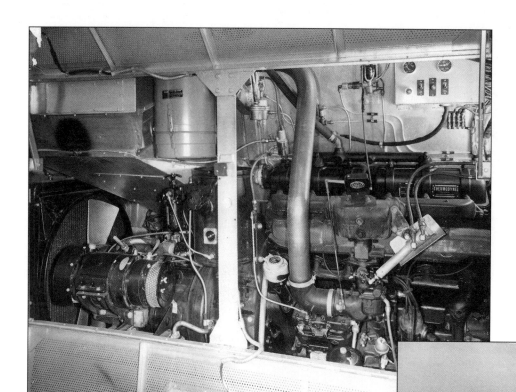

Shown here are the motor compartment and angle drive from the C33 experimental bus. The EN510A gasoline shown developed 158 hp and was a popular motor for buses, trucks, and fire apparatus. All had updraft carbs, but the fire truck versions also had dual ignition.

C33(916)547 C1111

C33-347V9798.

The C33 experimental bus is shown without motor and running gear.

This 1948 two-tone C33 diesel transit was delivered to Pierro & Sons, Jersey City, NJ. Only 9 C33s were diesel powered.

This 1948 C33DT required no clutch pedal due to the torque converter drive. The shift lever shown has three positions: reverse, neutral, and forward. The dash decal cautions the driver to shift into neutral before leaving his seat.

252 C37 buses were delivered between 1948 and 1953. 97 were EN510A gasoline powered and 155 were END510 diesels. This 1951 two-tone C37DT was one of two delivered to Debolt Transit Co., Homestead, PA.

This 1953 C37DT is an export model and has different front-end trim and emblem than the one shown on the preceding page.

576 C50s were delivered between 1950 and 1955, and were the "battleships" of Mack's post WWII offerings. These big 50 passenger transits had ENDS672 diesel powerplants, a 272-inch wheelbase, and both 96 and 102-inch widths. Overall length was 39 feet, 11 inches. This 1951 C50DT was delivered to the Cincinnati Street Railway Co.

Three C50DTs are posed prior to delivery to Toronto Transp. Commission. These were equipped with power steering and had a sharp turning radius.

No, the negative is not reversed. This is a 1949 prototype C50DT with right hand drive for export to Sweden, equipped with extra wide front doors.

400 of these C50DTs went to NYC in 1950 and 1951. These "biggies" rode on HD spoke wheels and were 96 inches wide.

Shown is a C50 under construction at Allentown plant 5C in 1951.

Mack built 10 rail motor cars for the New Haven Railroad between 1951 and 1954. These FCD rail buses were based on the C50 bus design, and weighed over 42,000 pounds. Mack built a total of 93 rail cars between 1905 and 1954.

519 C47 buses were built between 1953 and 1960. These 45 passenger buses were similar to the C45, but of lighter weight design. The Mack END673 diesel with a single combustion chamber and direct fuel injection was first used in the C47 bus. Adding a turbocharger raised horsepower from 170 to 205. The bus shown here is a 1957 C47DT, one of 10 delivered to Pittsburgh Railway Co. Because of the hills traversed, electric sanders can be seen forward of the rear wheels.

This 1959 C47DT was delivered to Denver Tramway Corp., and has a vastly different front-end treatment from the C47DT on the preceding page. This "new look" front end was devised by Niagara Frontier Transit System and was used on most Macks delivered in 1959.

1,409 C49 models were delivered from 1954 through 1960, and along with the C47 models, represented Mack's "last hurrah" in the transit bus market. These 50 passenger buses were a lighter weight version of the C50 and were available in both 96 and 102-inch widths. A 1954 C49DT is shown with disc wheels and front and rear entrance doors.

This 1959 C49DT is one of 450 delivered to San Francisco Municipal Railway between 1955 and 1959, and was the largest bus order ever for Mack.

Air suspension was introduced as an option in 1955 on the C49. Details of this rear suspension are shown here along with a photo of the motor compartment showing the ENDT673 motor, Spicer torque converter, and Leece Neville alternator with triple fan belts. This motor was available in both non-turbo (170 hp) and turbo versions (205 hp).

This is one of 30 C49DMs delivered to Pacific Greyhound in 1957, and 4 were delivered to Richmond Greyhound. They were of the single door type with transit type seating. Power was a Mack END673 diesel driving through a 4-speed TR91 manual transmission. One of these has survived and was acquired by the Pacific Bus Museum in 1999 and became part of their museum fleet.

Sadly, this C49DM for the Pennsylvania Department of Health was the last bus order accepted by Mack before exiting the bus business. This bus was shipped from Allentown, PA, on Jan. 25, 1960. The last C49 bus shipped was a San Francisco unit on Jan. 27, 1960, and the very last bus shipped was a C47 for Puerto Rico on Feb. 17, 1960. From 1945 through 1960 over 7,000 C model buses were produced.

Spurred by the Justice Department's antitrust action against GM and its largest bus customers, and encouragement from Greyhound, Mack built a prototype 40-foot, three axle, intercity bus for Greyhound Lines in 1957. It was dubbed a MV-620-D and ran in regular Greyhound service from 1958 through 1960. Neither Greyhound, nor anyone else ordered this coach, and in what had to be one of Mack's biggest disappointments ever, the MV-620-D became a "one-of-a-kind" vehicle. In July of 1999, this coach was donated to "America on Wheels, a Museum of Over the Road Transportation" to be built in Allentown, PA, and is slated to open in the year 2001. Hopefully, this coach will be preserved and displayed at this location only a few miles from where it was first conceived and built.

Serial #MV-620-D-1001

 Conceived, Designed and Built by
MACK TRUCKS, INC.

The Million Dollar Bus

(Unofficial name given to coach by Mack employees)

BUILT: Allentown, Pennsylvania
Initial design to delivery time: 9 months
Structural Assembly began August 12, 1957

OFFICIAL SHOWING TO GREYHOUND: Sidney, Ohio
December 4, 1957

PLACED IN REGULAR LINE SERVICE: March 11, 1958, as
Central Greyhound Lines #C-620 between
Chicago and Los Angeles or San Francisco via Salt Lake

LENGTH: 40 Feet

WIDTH: 8 Feet

HEIGHT: 11 Feet

EMPTY WEIGHT: 32,200 Pounds

ENGINE: Original-Mack 6 cylinder ENDLT-674
(Current-Mack V-8 ENDT-865)

TRANSMISSION: Original-Mack TRDL725 - 5 speed primary
and 2 speed compound
(Currently - straight 5 speed)

FUEL CAPACITY: 150 Gallons

ORIGINAL MACK DESIGNATION: MV 39-4572

FINAL/CURRENT DESIGNATION EXPLANATION: MV-620-D
M = Mack   V = Vision Liner
6 = Six wheels (dual wheels not counted)
2 = Two drive wheels
O = Original model   D = Diesel

SEATING CAPACITY: 39 - Level Floor

LAVATORY: Left rear corner of interior

TURNING RADIUS: 40 Feet (diameter 80 feet)

SUSPENSION: Mack Airglide

ROYAL COACH
911 CONLEY DRIVE, MECHANICSBURG, PA 17055 • (717) 691-1147

Built for Greyhound as part of a demonstration project fully funded by Mack, the MV-620-D operated in regular Greyhound line service from 1958 through 1960 between Chicago, San Francisco, and Los Angeles via Salt Lake City. In addition to the MV-620, the project included a PD 4104 and two (2) PD 4501's powered with a complete Mack drive train.

The MV-620 project was considered an engineering success. However, the demonstration was abruptly terminated in 1960 after a change in Greyhound senior management occurred. Subsequently, Greyhound became deeply involved with MCI, developing the MC-5, MC-6 and MC-7. The Mack project provided a platform of learning that was utilized later by Greyhound and Motor Coach Industries.

In 1964, Schenectady Street Railway (NY) purchased the MV-620 from Mack and painted it cream and green for their charter affiliate "Nation Wide Tours." The MV-620 saw service throughout the U.S. until 1969 when it was sold to George Kistler, Jr., Inc., a fire equipment sales company in Allentown, Pennsylvania, who utilized the coach for company transportation.

Mack Trucks, Inc. regained ownership of the MV-620 in 1972, placing the coach in company service as Bulldog Surface Lines. Initially Mack painted the coach black, white, and gold. In 1974, in preparation for the 1976 Bicentennial, the MV-620 was painted white, including the bright metal below the beltline, accented with red and blue paint, and Mack logos. The coach was easily recognized! It attracted attention traveling throughout the Northeast on company trips until 1985. After this time, the coach was used in local area company service around Mack World Headquarters in Allentown, Pennsylvania. In 1988, it was determined to have outlived its usefulness for the Mack organization.

During 1990, Mack Trucks, Inc. sold the MV-620. The coach is now part of the Royal Coach collection and is maintained by Wolf's Bus Lines, Inc., York Springs, Pennsylvania. Its final public showing in the Mack patriotic paint scheme was at the September 1990 Fall Bus Bash East.

Today, the MV-620 proudly displays its original two-tone blue, black, white, and gold Greyhound paint design and markings. Extensive body restoration work and painting was accomplished by Bill Shoop (Coach and Truck Refinishing), Reedsville, Pennsylvania. Its original destination roll sign is in place including the points the coach served while in Greyhound Service, the white dog logo on blue, SPECIAL, CHARTER, the Nation Wide Tours signs, the black MACK letters on white, and the Bulldog Surface Lines sign.

Future use of the MV-620, although maintained to current charter coach standards, will be limited to display at activities associated with the Motor Coach Industry and restored vehicles functions.

Photos and information relating to past activity of the coach will be greatly appreciated as Royal Coach is maintaining historical records of the MV-620.

Charles Wotring, owner of Royal Coach in Mechanicsburg, PA, bought the MV-620-D from Mack Trucks Inc. in 1990, and had it restored to its original condition and livery. Before donating the coach to the "America on Wheels" museum in 1999, the owner compiled the above detailed history and specifications, which are reprinted with permission. It is indeed, a happy occurrence that this unique, one-of-a-kind vehicle has been restored and preserved.

The modern styling of the period is reflected in the modest rear fins shown in this 1957 factory photo.

From 1974 to 1990, while owned by Mack, this rather gaudy 1976 bicentennial paint scheme was used. This coach is the only known example of any U.S. manufacturer's true one-of-a-kind, pilot, prototype/concept coach that is fully roadworthy today.

ADS-1 — 1156 C10221

The ADS-1 experimental bus of 1956 never reached the production stage (see previous photo on page 9). Many front and side shots of this bus have been published, but this rear view is seldom seen.

This handsome 97D intercity bus was built in Sidney, OH, in 1958 in the former C.D. Beck Co. plant. Only 26 were made and Mack was not able to overcome the stranglehold the GM PD4104 had on the American intercity bus market at the time.

The 97D was powered by the Mack ENDT673 diesel and had a 4-speed transmission. Despite their good looks and sturdy construction, they failed to sell in numbers necessary to sustain production.

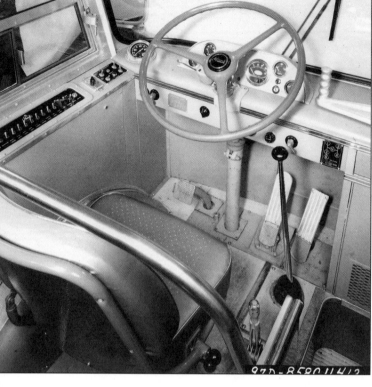

The spacious entranceway and driver's area are shown. The dashboard and instruments reflect the Beck bus heritage and show a great similarity to those also used in the C model Mack fire apparatus. The shift pattern for the 4-speed transmission is shown.

More Titles from Iconografix:

*This product is sold under license from Mack Trucks, Inc. Mack is a registered Trademark of Mack Trucks, Inc. All rights reserved.

All Iconografix books are available from direct mail specialty book dealers and bookstores worldwide, or can be ordered from the publisher. For book trade and distribution information or to add your name to our mailing list contact:

Iconografix, PO Box 446, Hudson, Wisconsin, 54016 Telephone: (715) 381-9755, (800) 289-3504 (USA), Fax: (715) 381-9756

NEW CAR CARRIERS
1910 - 1998 PHOTO ALBUM

Donald F. Wood

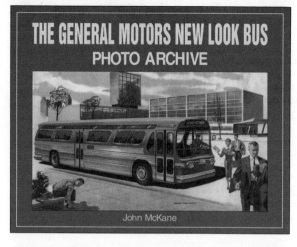

THE GENERAL MOTORS NEW LOOK BUS
PHOTO ARCHIVE

John McKane

MORE
GREAT BOOKS FROM
ICONOGRAFIX

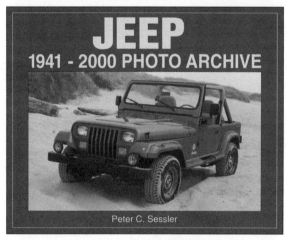

JEEP
1941 - 2000 PHOTO ARCHIVE

Peter C. Sessler

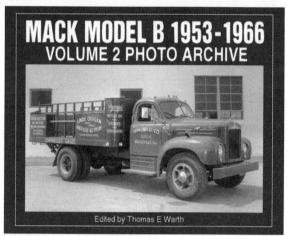

MACK MODEL B 1953-1966
VOLUME 2 PHOTO ARCHIVE

Edited by Thomas E Warth

LOGGING TRUCKS
1915-1970 PHOTO ARCHIVE

Donald F. Wood

MACK TRUCKS
PHOTO GALLERY

Edited by Thomas E. Warth

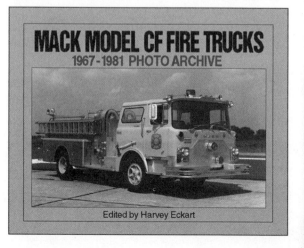

MACK MODEL CF FIRE TRUCKS
1967-1981 PHOTO ARCHIVE

Edited by Harvey Eckart